"Brian Fisher, Matt Morton, and Blake Jennings have done small-group leaders and participants a great service. Their studies of biblical characters use well-written questions to lead the discussion from observing Scripture texts to understanding and applying them. I hope this is only the beginning of a treasure trove of small-group Bible-study materials from these authors!"

—MARK H. HEINEMANN, professor of Christian education,
Dallas Theological Seminary

"A good set of character Bible studies is hard to find. The ORDINARY GREATNESS series is a solid tool for spiritual growth."

—DARRELL BOCK, research professor of New Testament Studies, professor of spiritual development and culture, Dallas Theological Seminary

"ORDINARY GREATNESS is a series that invites people to know the Word of God thoroughly, interpret it accurately, and apply it passionately. This is a key resource for anyone looking to break new ground in their knowledge of the Bible and their intimacy with the Lord."

—TIMOTHY ATEEK, director, Vertical Ministries

"Change is inevitable, but the right kind of change is special. God is the agent of lasting change in our lives. This series will help identify the changes God wants to make in you by showing you the changes He has made in biblical heroes. Brian, Matt, and Blake can lead you well because they have been led themselves by the Lord."

—GREGG MATTE, pastor, Houston's First Baptist Church;
founder, Breakaway Ministries

"Our twenty-first-century popular culture seems to ignore the need for rock-solid character growth. Brian, Matt, and Blake take us on a journey with three very human biblical men—Daniel, Gideon, and Peter—and show us how they grew into giants of the faith. This well-crafted series brings the Bible alive through lots of Scripture, opportunities for self-discovery, relevant stories, and a bias toward application."

studei  it,
ru

D1508799

BRIAN FISHER
MATT MORTON
BLAKE JENNINGS

DANIEL
STANDING STRONG IN A HOSTILE WORLD

TH1NK

TH1NK, an
Imprint of
NavPress

NAVPRESS

Discipleship Inside Out®

NavPress is the publishing ministry of The Navigators, an international Christian organization and leader in personal spiritual development. NavPress is committed to helping people grow spiritually and enjoy lives of meaning and hope through personal and group resources that are biblically rooted, culturally relevant, and highly practical.

**For a free catalog go to www.NavPress.com
or call 1.800.366.7788 in the United States or 1.800.839.4769 in Canada.**

Contents

Acknowledgments

WE WOULD LIKE to thank the many people who helped us complete this Bible study. Thank you to our wives, who supported and encouraged us during a frenetic year of simultaneous preaching and writing. Thank you to the wonderful elders and staff of Grace Bible Church, who gave us the time to write. Special thanks to Alyssa Luff, our research assistant for this study, and to Taylor Morgan, who drew the excellent sketch of Daniel's vision, which we have included in lesson 8.

How to Use This Study

THROUGH NO FAULT of their own, four young men named Daniel, Hananiah, Mishael, and Azariah found themselves as slaves, marching along a dusty road, moving away from their families, their homes, and their culture. Away from everything stable and secure, toward an uncertain future. How would they respond now that no one was watching? Would they stand up for God's truth and God's values, or would they play it safe and simply seek to blend in?

Studying the lives of these young men will change the way you think about God and His greatness, your own identity, and the opportunities you have even in the midst of difficult circumstances. Daniel and his friends stood out in the crowd—sometimes quite literally. Occasionally this brought praise, and at other times it brought persecution. However, whether they received praise or persecution, they each remained faithful to God. As a result, they had a profound impact on the foreign culture in which they lived.

Studying God's Word has the potential to transform us in amazing ways if we approach it with obedient hearts and open minds. The best environment for any Bible study is a small group of friends with whom you can discuss the questions and passages. We learn best when we have other people to encourage us and to hold us accountable. If you do this study with a group, answer the questions on your own throughout the week and then get together with your friends to discuss what you have learned and to encourage one another to live it out.

Each lesson is divided into four main sections. First, you will find introductory comments and two or three questions designed to get you thinking about the relevant topic for that week. The second section, called "Look It Over," will ask you to make basic observations about the week's Bible passage. Third, "Think It Through" will take you a bit deeper into questions about the passage's meaning for the original audience and its relevance for us. Finally, "Make It Real" will challenge you to apply the passage to your own life. Throughout the lessons you'll find one or two personal download applications. You'll be able to recognize them by the following download icon. Try not to skip these activities because they'll challenge you to really examine yourself and the main points of the week. At the end of each lesson there is a memory verse, chosen so that you can keep the main point of the lesson on your heart and mind throughout the week. If you are short on time one week, ask your leader which portions of the study will be most valuable for the group discussion.

You'll notice that every lesson includes the full text of the main Scripture reading(s), but you'll want to have a Bible or Bible app handy to look up the additional passages referenced throughout the lessons. Be sure to bring your Bible to your group meeting so you can discuss these passages with your friends.

Daniel is an amazingly dense book, packed with stirring stories and soaring prophetic visions. We have highlighted several key events and themes, but we encourage you to read and study the entire book. If you would like more information about Bible study methods or would like to download additional curricula, check us out online at www.grace-bible.org.

Brian Fisher, Matt Morton, and Blake Jennings

Why Me, God?

Those who suffer according to God's will should commit themselves to their faithful Creator and continue to do good.

1 PETER 4:19

DURING MY (BRIAN'S) senior year of high school, our district began competitive soccer for the first time. Several of my friends decided to try out for the team, so I tried out as well. I made the team, but no one told me how much running we would do! We ran to warm up; we ran during practice; we ran at the end of practice. Sprints and more sprints, miles and more miles. Our coach had never played soccer, but he knew a lot about conditioning, and he knew a lot about motivating teamwork. I vividly recall the first (and only) time some of the guys slacked off during practice. We all suffered for their laziness. At the end of practice, our coach made us all run an extra six miles. As you can imagine, those of us who gave our best effort weren't very happy with the slackers.

Daniel and his three friends faced a similar situation, but the consequences were so much worse. Although they personally had done nothing wrong, their freedom was gone. They were forced to march nine hundred miles from their home, and they were enslaved in a foreign land, all because of the sins of other people. And for the record, they never saw their homeland again. How would you have responded in those circumstances? Would you have felt angry? Bitter? Resentful toward those who had put you in such a terrible position? Or would you have accepted your circumstances, or even given thanks? Whether we find ourselves in difficult circumstances because of our own choices or the choices of someone else, God can teach us profound lessons. He can shape our character if we respond with wisdom. Read Daniel 1:1-4.

> In the third year of the reign of Jehoiakim king of Judah, Nebuchadnezzar king of Babylon came to Jerusalem and besieged it. And the Lord delivered Jehoiakim king of Judah into his hand, along with some of the articles from the temple of God. These he carried off to the temple of his god in Babylonia and put in the treasure house of his god.
>
> Then the king ordered Ashpenaz, chief of his court officials, to bring in some of the Israelites from the royal family and the nobility—young men without any physical defect, handsome, showing aptitude for every kind of learning, well informed, quick to understand, and qualified to serve in the king's palace. He was to teach them the language and literature of the Babylonians.

VALUE IN SUFFERING

1. List the most difficult or frustrating circumstances you have encountered. Who or what caused the difficulty (you, someone else, or no one in particular)?

2. How did you respond when the difficulty first began? Did your attitude, perspective, or behavior change with time? Why or why not?

>>>

THE PROBLEM OF SUFFERING

Daniel wasn't the only Jew who wondered about God's justice during the Babylonian exile. One of Daniel's contemporaries was the prophet Habakkuk. He questioned why God would use the wicked nation of Babylon to judge the comparatively righteous nation of Israel. Habakkuk exclaimed to God, "Your eyes are too pure to look on evil; you cannot tolerate wrong. Why then do you tolerate the treacherous? Why are you silent while the wicked [that is, the Babylonians] swallow up those more righteous than themselves [that is, the Jews]?" (Habakkuk 1:13). Both Habakkuk and Daniel learned that God's justice can always be trusted.

LOOK IT OVER

3. Examine Daniel 1:1-4 carefully. What are the key words and events that seem particularly important in order to understand the story? Summarize the main point of the passage in your own words.

   a. Key words:

b. Key events:

c. Main idea:

On the following page, you will find a timeline of some key events in Israel's history. This will help you to place the story of Daniel and his friends in the appropriate historical setting. Study it carefully before you continue with the rest of this lesson.

4. Why did Jehoiakim and the Jews lose their war against Nebuchadnezzar and the Babylonians (see 2 Kings 24:1-4)? What role did military strength and strategy play in their defeat? Could God have delivered His people from military defeat? How do you know?

5. Read Hebrews 12:7-11. For what purposes does God discipline His people? (Note: Another way to translate the Greek word for "discipline" is "train.")

A History of Israel's Exile and Return[1]

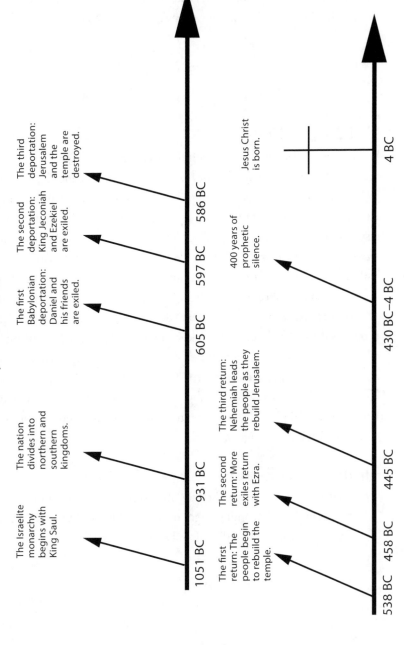

6. Read Hebrews 12:1-6. What attitudes, perspectives, and beliefs can help us to endure when we are suffering hardship?

IS GOD JUST?

Daniel and his friends came from influential families, maybe even from the royal family. As a result, they were certainly influenced by King Josiah's national revival (see 2 Kings 22–23). During this revival, young King Josiah led the Jewish nation away from sin and toward a deeper respect for and obedience to God. Daniel, Hananiah, Mishael, and Azariah were certainly aware of the blessings of obedience to God. They had also received education and training in the Law of Moses, and they knew well the prophecies of Isaiah and Jeremiah.

Twenty years before they were deported to Babylon, Jeremiah prophesied that God's people would be removed from the land because of their idolatry and lack of submission to His law (see Jeremiah 20:4-5; 25:1-13). Isaiah had even predicted that members of the Jewish royal family would serve the king of Babylon (see Isaiah 39:1-7). The book of Daniel begins in 605 BC, at the pinnacle of Babylonian power and the demise of Jewish sovereignty.

THINK IT THROUGH

7. How were Daniel and his friends able to accept their circumstances without becoming angry or bitter? What did they believe about God that helped them (see Daniel 2:19-22)?

Read James 1:2-4. Sometimes we suffer because of our own foolish choices, sometimes we suffer because of the choices of others, and sometimes we don't even know why we're suffering. Notice that James said nothing about the cause of our trials. Apparently James was more concerned with our *response* to trials than with the *reasons* for them.

8. What did James mean when he said, "Consider it pure joy"?

9. Is "joy" the same as "happiness"? How are they similar and how are they different?

MAKE IT REAL

If anybody understood hardship, Corrie ten Boom did. Corrie was a Dutch Christian who lived through the horrors of World War II. During the war, she and her family sheltered many Jews in a secret room, saving them from certain death at the hands of the Nazis. However, they were eventually discovered, and the entire family was sent to Scheveningen Prison. Corrie's father died there, and she and her sister Betsie were later transferred to Ravensbrück, a concentration camp near Berlin. Eventually Betsie died as well, leaving Corrie to carry on while bearing her grief and pain.[2]

Despite the terrible chain of events, Corrie ten Boom didn't waste her remaining years wallowing in bitterness and anger. Instead, she invested her life in preaching God's forgiveness through Jesus Christ. At one point she even had the opportunity to grant forgiveness, face-to-face, to one of her former concentration camp guards![3] She is a vivid illustration of how we can "consider it pure joy" even in the midst of difficult trials.

10. How can you "count it all joy" in the midst of hard circumstances? What actions can you take and what mind-set can you embrace so that you not only endure but overcome?

11. What happens to you and others around you when you persevere through trials?

12. What happens to you and others around you when you refuse to "consider it pure joy" in the midst of difficult circumstances?

List at least five reasons for having joy in the midst of difficult circumstances.

MEMORIZE

For this week, memorize James 1:2-4:

> **Consider it pure joy, my brothers, whenever you face trials of many kinds, because you know that the testing of your faith develops perseverance. Perseverance must finish its work so that you may be mature and complete, not lacking anything.**

If you are doing this study with a group, recite these verses to one another at the start of your next group discussion. Each week, add the new verse or verses to the ones you've already memorized to make sure that you remember them.

Hello, My Name Is . . .

Jesus took one look up and said, "You're John's son, Simon?
From now on your name is Cephas" (or Peter, which means
"Rock").

JOHN 1:42, MSG

A NAME OR A NUMBER?

During World War II, the Nazis created concentration camps to house,
and ultimately to exterminate, the Jewish race. Every Jewish man,
woman, and child was assigned a number, which was tattooed onto his
or her wrist. Never would the Nazis call the Jews by their names, only by
their numbers. Why? Because according to Nazi ideology, the Jews were
less than human. Nazis intended to communicate to the Jews in every
possible way, "You are nothing more than a number. You don't have
individual value. You are not related to others in any meaningful way."

This world, which is hostile to God, will always try to rename us. In
extreme cases, the world might even reduce us to a number. It will spare
no effort to reclassify us as something less than God's highest order of
creation, made in His image, designed to reflect His glory. The world
will attempt to create a new identity for us, one consistent with its own
values and priorities.

Daniel and his friends were given names at birth that reflected their parents' faith in the one true God, the maker of heaven and earth. Later, the names of these young men represented their own growing faith as well. But after the young men were separated from their families and uprooted from the culture that supported their faith, the Babylonian authorities assigned them new names. They were forced to make a decision: Would they accept the Babylonian identities and beliefs associated with their new names, or would they remain true to God? Read Daniel 1:3-7:

> Then the king ordered Ashpenaz, chief of his court officials, to bring in some of the Israelites from the royal family and the nobility—young men without any physical defect, handsome, showing aptitude for every kind of learning, well informed, quick to understand, and qualified to serve in the king's palace. He was to teach them the language and literature of the Babylonians. The king assigned them a daily amount of food and wine from the king's table. They were to be trained for three years, and after that they were to enter the king's service.
>
> Among these were some from Judah: Daniel, Hananiah, Mishael and Azariah. The chief official gave them new names: to Daniel, the name Belteshazzar; to Hananiah, Shadrach; to Mishael, Meshach; and to Azariah, Abednego.

THE IMPORTANCE OF NAMES

Many parents these days name their children without much thought. They buy a book of names, or they name their child after their favorite celebrity. But in biblical times, Jewish parents took their children's names very seriously. Names reflected their faith in God or their hopes and dreams for the future. It wasn't uncommon for a person to be renamed because of a significant event, accomplishment, or decision. God was the first "namer" in history. He gave Adam his name. He was also the first "renamer," changing Abram's name to Abraham. In other words, names have *meaning*; they aren't just *sounds*. Look at some of these biblical names from the book of Daniel and their meanings in Hebrew or Chaldean:

- Daniel = "My Judge is El (God)"
    Belteshazzar = "Nebo, protect his life!"
- Hananiah = "Yahweh has shown grace"
    Shadrach = "The Command of Aku (moon-god)"
- Mishael = "Who is what God is?"
    Meshach = "Who is what Aku is?"
- Azariah = "Yahweh (The Lord) has helped"
    Abednego = "Servant of Nego (Nebo)"
- Nebuchadnezzar = "Nebo, protect my boundary!"[1]

WHO ARE YOU?

1. What does your name mean? Take a minute to look it up; you might be surprised by what you find. Do you think your name reflects who you are or hope to be? If you had the chance to rename yourself in a way that reflected what you most value about yourself, or the person you hope to become, what name would you choose?

My name:

Meaning:

Name I would choose:

Meaning:

Why I would choose that name:

2. If your friends were to rename you, what names do you think
   they would choose? Do you think they really know you? Why or
   why not?

Part of knowing who you are is knowing what you stand for and
what you believe. A worldview is a set of ideas or beliefs about the basic
truths of reality and the important questions of life. For example: "Do
we gain truth through our senses, our feelings, or from God?" "What is
a human being? Was he created or did he evolve?" "How do we tell right
from wrong?" "What is real (only what we see, or unseen things as well)?"
"What happens to us when we die?"

Each of us has a worldview, whether we're aware of it or not. We use
our worldview every day to interpret and interact with the world. It's like
a pair of glasses through which we see the world. Each of our glasses is
unique to some degree—we don't see everything exactly as our family,
friends, coworkers, or any other person on the planet. Many of us don't
think about our worldview, but it significantly affects how we understand the world and make decisions.

3. Think about how you spend your time, money, and energy.
   Also consider the subjects you discuss most often and the people

you admire. Based on your personal reflection, what would you say you value (grades, money, friends, dating, or something else)? Make a list of your values here.

4. Where do you get your values? From other people? From within yourself? From God and His Word?

LOOK IT OVER

The ruins of ancient Babylon are situated about fifty miles south of modern-day Baghdad in Iraq, along the Euphrates River. This ancient city was the capital of an empire that stretched from modern-day Kuwait through Iraq, southern Turkey, Syria, and even into Egypt.[2] It was a vast and powerful ancient empire.

Under the reign of Nebuchadnezzar, Babylon, whose name means "the gate of god(s)," achieved immense opulence and grandeur. The king constructed a city covering 3.2 square miles (approximately two thousand acres), surrounded by two walls—the outer wall was twenty-one feet thick, and the inner wall was twelve.[3] The two walls were separated by a military road twenty-three feet wide.[4] Palaces and temples to false gods filled the city, and many of the buildings within the walls were covered with enamel tiles of yellow, white, and blue that radiantly reflected the sun.[5]

Nebuchadnezzar considered himself a god on earth. He was proud of himself and of his city. According to Daniel 4, God disciplined the king's pride by causing him to lose his mind. For a time, the king thought he was an animal, living outdoors and eating grass like a cow.

Based on Babylon's historical significance, biblical writers often chose Babylon as a symbol of this fallen world's values, which oppose God and His will (see Revelation 14:8; 17:5).

5. What does Babylon represent in the following verses? What are we warned against?

- Isaiah 13:19

- Isaiah 21:9

- Habakkuk 1:5-11,15-17; 2:6,9,12,15,19

- Revelation 14:8

- Revelation 18:1-19

Babylon wanted to seduce the rest of the world to embrace her worldview—her ways were fulfilling, her values best, her concept of the "good life" enduring and untouchable. When Daniel recorded that he and his friends were taught "the language and literature," he wasn't referring to just a volume of books in a foreign language, but to an entirely new and ungodly worldview. Daniel 1:4 in *The Message* accurately reflects this understanding: "Indoctrinate them in the Babylonian language and the lore of magic and fortunetelling."

The "wise men" of Babylon made advances in art, literature, mathematics, and science, but the foundation of their educational and ethical system stood in direct opposition to the one true God. Astrology undergirded their entire way of thinking about themselves and their world. Their false gods had arranged the stars, and that arrangement determined the course of men's lives. The prophet Isaiah characterized the pride with which the Babylonians promoted their worldview: "I am, and there is none besides me" (Isaiah 47:10).

This new system of thinking was forced upon Daniel, Hananiah, Mishael, and Azariah. In much the same way, our culture tries to train us each day to conform our thinking to its own so that we'll think of others and ourselves according to its rules.

6. On what basis did King Nebuchadnezzar select the men who would serve him most closely?

- What does the king's criteria for service tell you about the demands of the job (serving in his court) and about the values of his culture?

- If you were selecting people to work for you or with you, what characteristics would be most important to you?

THINK IT THROUGH

The Jewish people are descendants of Noah's son Shem. The name Shem actually means "name." Names are significant—even the name "Name"! To this day, Jewish people revere the name of God so highly that they will not pronounce His personal name (represented by the four Hebrew letters YHWH). Instead, they call Him "The Name" because He is the name above all names. And what is more, the "name" of the Jewish people was derived from His name (see 2 Chronicles 7:14). It was their calling (as it was the calling of the first inhabitants of the earth, and it is now our calling as believers in Jesus Christ) to "make a name" for God, to make His character and reputation famous in all of the earth. It was unthinkable that they would be called by the name of another god or spend their lives making a name for another god. They were created and called for God's glory alone.

7. Why did the Babylonians rename these four young men?

8. Why did they use the names of their own gods in the new names they assigned?

9. What do "gods" represent in a culture?

10. What are the "gods" of your culture?

MAKE IT REAL

11. Through His Word, God has given us several fundamental truths that should shape the way we see ourselves, others, our circumstances, the future, and reality itself. Look at the passages below and write down the truth each one presents to us:

* Genesis 1:1,26-27

* Romans 3:23

* Ephesians 2:8-9

* 1 Corinthians 6:11

* Colossians 3:12

- Romans 8:28

12. What happens to people when they reject these fundamental truths (see Psalm 14:1-3; Romans 1:21; Ephesians 4:17-19)?

What "names" do you feel pressured by our culture to accept? Check all that apply.

☐ Youngest
☐ Best-looking
☐ Strongest
☐ Smartest
☐ Richest
☐ Most powerful
☐ Most popular
☐ Most famous
☐ Highest social status
☐ Funniest
☐ Other: _____

Have you accepted your culture's "name" for you? Why or why not? How do you know?

How can you think and act consistently with God's understanding of your identity (see Romans 8:5-11)?

MEMORIZE

Review last week's verses, and then memorize 1 Peter 2:9:

But you are a chosen people, a royal priesthood, a holy nation, a people belonging to God, that you may declare the praises of him who called you out of darkness into his wonderful light.

No Compromise

Slaves, obey your earthly masters in everything; and do it, not only when their eye is on you and to win their favor, but with sincerity of heart and reverence for the Lord.

COLOSSIANS 3:22

CONFESSIONS OF A TEENAGE SLACKER

Like many teenagers, our friend Matt Irwin mowed his lawn in order to earn a weekly allowance from his father. His house had a large, hilly lawn, which Matt cut using a gas-powered, push lawn mower.

In time, Matt noticed that his dad did not inspect one part of the lawn on a regular basis. The south end of the lawn was invisible from the house because it was at the bottom of a steep hill. In addition, Matt's father consistently left the house from a door that led to the north.

In an epiphany of youthful ingenuity, Matt devised a scheme to minimize his workload while still claiming his entire allowance. He mowed only the extreme southern end of the lawn every few weeks, counting on the fact that his father would never notice the tall grass lurking at the bottom of the hill . . . and, of course, he would eventually get the job done. That worked for a while, until after four weeks of Matt's avoiding his duty, his dad went to the backyard to train his bird dog.

When the dog disappeared in the high grass to retrieve a rubber training bird, Matt's deceitful plan was exposed.

In Matt's own words, "He didn't yell; he didn't even put on a stern face. He calmly looked at me and said, 'Come with me.' I followed. He stopped, completely silent, as we both surveyed the crime scene. I'm telling you, that willfully uncut patch of lawn looked about twelve feet high at that moment. He then turned to me and simply said, 'You've been cheating me—*and* yourself, as you'll soon realize, but starting now, you'll pay us both back. You will mow the rest of this lawn. You won't come back inside until it looks as perfect as what you've done elsewhere. And you will use these.' He held out a pair of fingernail clippers."

Four hours later, clipping away in the darkness, Matt had cleared only about one square meter of the lawn with his pitifully inadequate tool. His dad graciously allowed him to cut the rest of the lawn with the mower the following morning. However, the lessons stuck with Matt for the rest of his life: Our character is revealed by how we act when we think nobody is watching, and shortcuts never pay off in the long run.

»»

ARE YOU *WHOLE*?

The word *integrity* comes from a Latin word meaning "untouched." Something untouched, or undamaged, is whole and complete. When applied to someone's character, the person with integrity is a complete person. The inner person is healthy and mature, and his internal character remains consistent with his external behavior in any and every circumstance. Do you have integrity?

1. Have you ever taken a shortcut at a job or on your schoolwork because you thought you wouldn't get caught? What did you hope to gain by taking the shortcut?

2. Have you ever compromised your moral values because you believed you could get away with it? How did you feel afterward?

DINING WITH THE DEVIL?

Because they were so far from their homes, Daniel and his friends could have rationalized any behavior by telling themselves, "No one will know." So far from the temple in Jerusalem, they could have reasoned, "God will not see." However, they intentionally chose to remain true to their values, regardless of who was watching. Read Daniel 1:5-6,8-16:

> The king assigned them a daily amount of food and wine from the king's table. They were to be trained for three years, and after that they were to enter the king's service.
>
> Among these were some from Judah: Daniel, Hananiah, Mishael and Azariah. . . .
>
> But Daniel resolved not to defile himself with the royal food and wine, and he asked the chief official for permission not to defile himself this way. Now God had caused the official to show favor and sympathy to Daniel, but the official told Daniel,

"I am afraid of my lord the king, who has assigned your food and drink. Why should he see you looking worse than the other young men your age? The king would then have my head because of you."

Daniel then said to the guard whom the chief official had appointed over Daniel, Hananiah, Mishael and Azariah, "Please test your servants for ten days: Give us nothing but vegetables to eat and water to drink. Then compare our appearance with that of the young men who eat the royal food, and treat your servants in accordance with what you see." So he agreed to this and tested them for ten days.

At the end of the ten days they looked healthier and better nourished than any of the young men who ate the royal food. So the guard took away their choice food and the wine they were to drink and gave them vegetables instead.

LOOK IT OVER

3. Examine Daniel 1:5-16 carefully. What are the key words and events that seem particularly important in order to understand the story? Summarize the main point of the passage in your own words.

   a. Key words:

   b. Key events:

c. Main idea:

4. Why was the chief official initially afraid to let Daniel and his friends avoid the king's food? What were the potential consequences for him and for Daniel and his friends? If you had been the chief official, would you have allowed the experiment to proceed?

5. Why did this dietary experiment have such positive results? Does this story teach us that we should all be vegetarians? Why or why not?

THINK IT THROUGH

For Daniel and his friends, eating the king's food and drinking his wine were spiritual and moral issues. Almost certainly the king's food and wine (1) included meat from animals that Jews were prohibited to eat (see Leviticus 11); (2) was prepared in such a way that it still included blood and fat (see Leviticus 3:17); and (3) had first been dedicated to idols, violating their understanding of the first two commandments of the Mosaic Law (see Exodus 20:3-4).

A Middle Eastern saying, "There is bread and salt between us," meant that a relationship had been confirmed by sharing a meal.[1] Sharing a meal symbolized a commitment to friendship and it communicated a sharing of values. For this reason, eating from the king's table wasn't just about food and drink—it was a statement about accepting or rejecting the king's values, morals, and worldview.

6. What does Daniel's response to the chief official (see Daniel 1:11-13) tell you about his character?

7. Why do you think this was such an important stand for Daniel and his friends to take?

8. What does the word *defile* mean? What comes to your mind from your own culture and experience when you hear the word *defile*?

9. What does it mean that Daniel resolved not to defile himself? Is "resolve" a feeling, an attitude, a choice, or something else? What do you suppose Daniel and his friends would have done if the diet had failed?

10. There are many ways we can and should respond to the temptation to compromise our values, depending on our specific circumstances. How did each person below respond to temptation, and why was each response appropriate? Did life always turn out "good" for these people who remained faithful to God?

- Joseph (see Genesis 39)

- Job (see Job 2:7-10)

- Jesus (see Matthew 16:21-23)

- Peter and the apostles (see Acts 4:18-23; 5:40-42)

MAKE IT REAL

How are you tempted to sacrifice your integrity when no one is watching or when no one is around to punish you for your compromise? Look at the following list of temptations and check the ones that cause you to struggle:

☐ Cheating on tests
☐ Viewing pornography

☐ Laziness
☐ Stealing
☐ Crossing boundaries with the opposite sex
☐ Drinking
☐ Gossiping about others
☐ Other: _____

"I'VE GOT MY EYE ON YOU!"

When I (Brian) was a kid, my dad told me this story:

> Tom was a crusty old farmer whose dairy farm was about three miles from our place and just one mile past my grandmother's farm. He always kind of growled at me and the other boys, but we knew down deep he liked us kids. We could come to his farm anytime, even when he was busy milking the cows. He would find jobs for us to do like cleaning out stalls or feeding calves. Then he would go off to do other things, but he would warn us that he would be watching us . . . and we believed him because Tom had one glass eye that he would remove, wash off in his mouth, and set on a fence post or shelf nearby. He claimed that through that glass eye, he could see everything we were doing. As we began to work, keeping one eye on Tom's eye, he would be around the corner watching us. Upon returning, he would tell us specific things about our work that he could know only if he had been watching. We were convinced: Tom could see us through that glass eye! Not surprisingly, knowing he was watching changed the way we did our work.

11. Read Jeremiah 23:24 (see also Psalm 94:9; 139). How does it make you feel knowing that God sees everything, not just our actions but even the motives of our hearts? Amazed, encouraged, afraid, indifferent, or something else? Why?

What is one concrete step you will take this week to align your private character with your public reputation? If you're comfortable sharing what you wrote, tell a trusted friend or mentor and ask him or her to follow up with you in a week about how it went.

MEMORIZE

Review last week's verse, and then memorize Colossians 3:23-24:

> **Whatever you do, work at it with all your heart, as working for the Lord, not for men, since you know that you will receive an inheritance from the Lord as a reward. It is the Lord Christ you are serving.**

Strength in Numbers

Saul's son Jonathan went to David at Horesh and helped him find strength in God.

1 SAMUEL 23:16

ONE OF THE most dramatic stories of Christian martyrdom occurred in AD 320 in Sebaste, a town located in the modern-day country of Turkey. The Roman emperor Licinius reversed his policy of religious freedom and began severely persecuting Christians throughout the eastern portions of his empire. Forty brave Roman soldiers refused to deny their faith in Jesus. As a result, they were condemned to die for treason.

Their general devised a particularly cruel method of execution. He ordered the offending soldiers to stand naked on a frozen lake in the middle of winter, where they would slowly and painfully freeze to death. He placed a warm tub of water at the edge of the lake and offered it to any soldier who would renounce his faith. The forty brave men rushed to the center of the ice, removed their clothes, and prayed that God would give all of them the strength to endure.

After several hours on the ice, one of the soldiers ran to the warm bath, recanting his confession of faith. The number on the ice was reduced to thirty-nine, but not for long. A soldier was warming himself by the bath, having been posted there to monitor the men standing on the ice. He was deeply moved by the courage and conviction of these faithful Christians and believed in Jesus as a result of their testimony. When he saw one man leave the ice, he took off his own clothes and joined his fellow believers on the frozen lake. He died, along with thirty-nine other Christians, because he refused to accept temporary comfort in exchange for eternal reward.

As tragic as this story may appear, in reality it stands as a record of courageous victory. To this day the Eastern Orthodox and Roman Catholic churches celebrate feast days dedicated to these brave and faithful men. Their story encourages Christians throughout the world. And most importantly, these men are now with their Savior, enjoying eternal reward and unspeakable joy.[1]

THE COURAGE TO TAKE A STAND

1. Do you think you would have stayed on the ice with the other soldiers? Why or why not?

2. Is there anything in your life for which you would sacrifice your comfort, your reputation, or even your life?

WE WON'T BOW DOWN!

Three of Daniel's young friends faced a situation similar to the martyrs of Sebaste when confronted with King Nebuchadnezzar's command to worship a ninety-foot idol. Read these selections from Daniel 3:

King Nebuchadnezzar made an image of gold, ninety feet high and nine feet wide, and set it up on the plain of Dura in the province of Babylon. . . . [Then] the satraps, prefects, governors, advisers, treasurers, judges, magistrates and all the other provincial officials assembled for the dedication of the image that King Nebuchadnezzar had set up, and they stood before it.

Then the herald loudly proclaimed, "This is what you are commanded to do, O peoples, nations and men of every language: As soon as you hear the sound of the horn, flute, zither, lyre, harp, pipes and all kinds of music, you must fall down and worship the image of gold that King Nebuchadnezzar has set up. Whoever does not fall down and worship will immediately be thrown into a blazing furnace."

Therefore, as soon as they heard the sound . . . of music, all the peoples, nations and men of every language fell down and worshiped the image of gold that King Nebuchadnezzar had set up.

At this time some astrologers came forward and denounced the Jews. They said to King Nebuchadnezzar, "O king, live forever! . . . There are some Jews whom you have set over the affairs of the province of Babylon — Shadrach, Meshach and Abednego — who pay no attention to you, O king. They neither serve your gods nor worship the image of gold you have set up."

Furious with rage, Nebuchadnezzar summoned Shadrach, Meshach and Abednego. So these men were brought before the king, and Nebuchadnezzar said to them, "Is it true, Shadrach, Meshach and Abednego, that you do not serve my gods or worship the image of gold I have set up? . . . If you do not worship it, you will be thrown immediately into a blazing furnace. Then what god will be able to rescue you from my hand?"

Shadrach, Meshach and Abednego replied to the king, "O Nebuchadnezzar, we do not need to defend ourselves before you in this matter. If we are thrown into the blazing furnace, the

God we serve is able to save us from it, and he will rescue us from your hand, O king. But even if he does not, we want you to know, O king, that we will not serve your gods or worship the image of gold you have set up." (verses 1,3-9,12-18)

LOOK IT OVER (PART 1)

3. Examine Daniel 3:1-18 carefully. What are the key words and events that seem particularly important in order to understand the story? Summarize the main point of the passage in your own words.

   a. Key words:

   b. Key events:

   c. Main idea:

4. Why did Shadrach, Meshach, and Abednego refuse to bow before the golden statue (see Exodus 20:1-5)?

5. What gave these three young men the courage to defy the king's order and to risk their lives?

MORE POWERFUL THAN KINGS

To put it mildly, the king wasn't pleased with the three friends' refusal to obey his orders. However, God is infinitely more powerful than any king, and He was there with our three heroes. Read Daniel 3:19-30:

> Then Nebuchadnezzar was furious with Shadrach, Meshach and Abednego, and his attitude toward them changed. He ordered the furnace heated seven times hotter than usual and commanded some of the strongest soldiers in his army to tie up Shadrach, Meshach and Abednego and throw them into the blazing furnace. So these men, wearing their robes, trousers, turbans and other clothes, were bound and thrown into the blazing furnace. The king's command was so urgent and the furnace so hot that the flames of the fire killed the soldiers who took up Shadrach, Meshach and Abednego, and these three men, firmly tied, fell into the blazing furnace.
>
> Then King Nebuchadnezzar leaped to his feet in amazement and asked his advisers, "Weren't there three men that we

tied up and threw into the fire?"

They replied, "Certainly, O king."

He said, "Look! I see four men walking around in the fire, unbound and unharmed, and the fourth looks like a son of the gods."

Nebuchadnezzar then approached the opening of the blazing furnace and shouted, "Shadrach, Meshach and Abednego, servants of the Most High God, come out! Come here!"

So Shadrach, Meshach and Abednego came out of the fire, and the satraps, prefects, governors and royal advisers crowded around them. They saw that the fire had not harmed their bodies, nor was a hair of their heads singed; their robes were not scorched, and there was no smell of fire on them.

Then Nebuchadnezzar said, "Praise be to the God of Shadrach, Meshach and Abednego, who has sent his angel and rescued his servants! They trusted in him and defied the king's command and were willing to give up their lives rather than serve or worship any god except their own God. Therefore I decree that the people of any nation or language who say anything against the God of Shadrach, Meshach and Abednego be cut into pieces and their houses be turned into piles of rubble, for no other god can save in this way."

Then the king promoted Shadrach, Meshach and Abednego in the province of Babylon.

LOOK IT OVER (PART 2)

6. Examine Daniel 3:19-30 carefully. What are the key words and events that seem particularly important in order to understand the story? Summarize the main point of the passage in your own words.

a. Key words:

b. Key events:

c. Main idea:

7. Look closely at the description of the three men in the second half of verse 27. Write down the details Daniel wrote about their appearance after they emerged from the furnace.

8. Describe the outcome of Shadrach, Meshach, and Abednego's courageous stand against the king (see verses 28-29).

THINK IT THROUGH

9. Why did Nebuchadnezzar require his leadership to bow down before the golden statue? What was the significance of this command?

》》》

A STATUE MADE OF FEAR

Although Daniel didn't explain why Nebuchadnezzar built an enormous golden idol, we can get a good idea of the reason when we read the book carefully. Daniel 2 recounts Daniel's interpretation of Nebuchadnezzar's dream. The king had a vision of a statue, which represented four powerful earthly kingdoms, one of which was Nebuchadnezzar's Babylonian empire. But a huge stone, representing God's eternal kingdom, destroyed the statue and filled the entire earth. In other words, Nebuchadnezzar's kingdom faced certain destruction at the hands of an all-powerful God. Out of fear and a desire to assert his authority, Nebuchadnezzar built a large golden statue to represent the power and might of Babylon. Forcing his leaders to bow before that statue was a way of expressing his rebellion against the plans God had revealed.

10. Why did the writer include such a detailed description of the men after they emerged from the fire (see verse 27 and question 7 on page 49)?

11. Who do you think was the fourth person Nebuchadnezzar saw walking around in the fire? How was he described? Where else in the Bible do you find other such descriptions of a man?

12. Do you think the three young men expected to be saved from the fire or not? If they expected to be saved, does that make their refusal to bow less impressive? Why or why not?

13. How did the following people encourage (or discourage) one another as they sought to follow God faithfully?

- Ruth and Naomi (see Ruth 1:16)

- Moses, Joshua, Aaron, and Hur (see Exodus 17:8-14)

- Joshua and Caleb (see Numbers 13:25–14:10)

- David and Jonathan (see 1 Samuel 18:1-4)

- Peter and John (see Acts 4:18-22; 5:40-42)

MAKE IT REAL

When we (Blake and Matt) started college, we both lived in a dorm on the campus of our secular university. We were surrounded, as were Daniel's three friends, with young men who made daily choices to disobey God. Sexual sin, drunkenness, violence, and disrespect toward authority seemed rampant among the people who surrounded us. It was often difficult to choose to honor the Lord in such a hostile environment.

We were fortunate, though, that we met one another and a handful of other strong Christian friends early in our college career. Although following Christ is difficult, it is immeasurably easier with the help of others who also want to do what is right. Our prayer for you is that you'll find a group of people who will encourage you to know God and obey Him.

Shadrach, Meshach, and Abednego drew some of their courage from their strong friendships. Do you have Christian friends who can encourage you to honor God with your actions? If so, write down one way in which you can practically help one another remain true to God. If you don't have a group of Christian friends, spend a few minutes in prayer asking God to provide some for you. Then, write down the names of a few people at school, church, or in this Bible study whom you will approach this week for encouragement, accountability, and prayer.

MEMORIZE

Review the previous weeks' verses, and then memorize Hebrews 10:24-25:

> **And let us consider how we may spur one another on toward love and good deeds. Let us not give up meeting together, as some are in the habit of doing, but let us encourage one another — and all the more as you see the Day approaching.**

Standing (and Kneeling) Alone

I issue a decree that in every part of my kingdom people must fear and reverence the God of Daniel. For he is the living God and he endures forever; his kingdom will not be destroyed, his dominion will never end.

DANIEL 6:26

I (BLAKE) HAD a close friendship in high school with a kind, popular, attractive girl who was not a Christian. Sarah (not her real name) lived a good life but simply refused to believe in the God of the Bible. I prayed for her salvation and tried to share my faith with her but often chickened out. I didn't want to risk offending her and losing our friendship. Unfortunately, one of our less-than-kind classmates, who was not a Christian either, saw in my friendship with Sarah an opportunity to publicly humiliate me for my faith. He knew what the Bible teaches about hell—that it's the judgment that awaits those who choose to reject the gospel. He knew that most of our classmates disagreed with that teaching and found it incredibly offensive. And so, as I chatted with Sarah in class one morning, he asked in a loud voice so that all our classmates could hear, "Blake, you believe Sarah is going to hell if she doesn't believe in Jesus, right?"

I was trapped. My heart began to race. My palms broke out in sweat. All eyes were on me, including Sarah's. I faced a painful choice. Would I take a stand for my belief in hell even if it made me unpopular and, worse, cost me my friendship with Sarah? Or would I deny my belief to save what little popularity I had and protect my relationship with her? Sadly, I can't remember what choice I made! The stress of that moment so overwhelmed me that today all I can remember is the pounding of my heart and the ringing of my ears! That proved to be one of the hardest moments of my high school years.

Daniel also faced a trap toward the end of his life, and the consequences of his decision were far, far greater. At more than eighty years old, Daniel began to serve the new king of Babylon, a man named Darius the Mede. Once again, Daniel distinguished himself among all the king's administrators. Based on Daniel's proven wisdom, faithfulness, and integrity, the new king decided to appoint him over the entire kingdom. But that honor made Daniel a target of his peers. Unable to catch him in corruption or incompetence, they set out to trap him in his faith.

It pleased Darius to appoint 120 satraps to rule throughout the kingdom, with three administrators over them, one of whom was Daniel. The satraps were made accountable to them so that the king might not suffer loss. Now Daniel so distinguished himself among the administrators and the satraps by his exceptional qualities that the king planned to set him over the whole kingdom. At this, the administrators and the satraps tried to find grounds for charges against Daniel in his conduct of government affairs, but they were unable to do so. They could find no corruption in him, because he was trustworthy and neither corrupt nor negligent. Finally these men said, "We will never find any basis for charges against this man Daniel unless it has something to do with the law of his God."

So the administrators and the satraps went as a group to the king and said: "O King Darius, live forever! The royal administrators, prefects, satraps, advisers and governors have all agreed that the king should issue an edict and enforce the decree that anyone who prays to any god or man during the next thirty days, except to you, O king, shall be thrown into the lions' den. Now, O king, issue the decree and put it in writing so that it cannot be altered—in accordance with the laws of the Medes and Persians, which cannot be repealed." So King Darius put the decree in writing. (Daniel 6:1-9)

IN THE LIONS' DEN

Many of us first heard the story of Daniel and the lions' den as children. Do you remember the cute, cartoonish pictures of lions from Sunday school? In reality, there's nothing cute about man-eating lions.

In 1898 the British set out to build a bridge over the river Tsavo in Kenya. Not long into the project, two man-eating lions began to stalk the camp. They attacked the tents in the dark of night, dragging their victims into the tall grass to devour them. Over a period of nine months, the lions killed between twenty-eight and one hundred men (accounts vary). Hundreds of workers fled the camp in fear. The deadliest of the lions measured nine feet eight inches and, when finally killed, required eight men to carry its carcass.[1]

With the lions of Tsavo in mind, we can better appreciate the trap that was set for Daniel. If he remained faithful to pray daily to the one true God, he would find himself face-to-face with the brutal power and killing efficiency of an entire pack of man-eating lions.

1. If you were in Daniel's shoes, in which of the following ways would you respond?

☐ I would wait a few weeks to pray. It's just not worth the risk.

☐ I'd still pray, but I'd do it privately. No sense inviting persecution.

☐ I'd pray in public for all to see. Bring on the lions!

Why? Be honest!

2. Have you ever had to suffer because you took a stand for your faith in Christ? If so, describe the situation.

DANIEL'S CHOICE AND GOD'S PROVISION

Look at Daniel's response to this life-or-death choice and the remarkable outcome of his decision:

When Daniel learned that the decree had been published, he went home to his upstairs room where the windows opened toward Jerusalem. Three times a day he got down on his knees and prayed, giving thanks to his God, just as he had done before. Then these men went as a group and found Daniel praying and asking God for help. So they went to the king and spoke to him about his royal decree: "Did you not publish a decree that during the next thirty days anyone who prays to any god or man except to you, O king, would be thrown into the lions' den?"

The king answered, "The decree stands—in accordance with the laws of the Medes and Persians, which cannot be repealed."

Then they said to the king, "Daniel, who is one of the exiles from Judah, pays no attention to you, O king, or to the decree you put in writing. He still prays three times a day." When the king heard this, he was greatly distressed; he was determined to rescue Daniel and made every effort until sundown to save him.

Then the men went as a group to the king and said to him, "Remember, O king, that according to the law of the Medes and Persians no decree or edict that the king issues can be changed."

So the king gave the order, and they brought Daniel and threw him into the lions' den. The king said to Daniel, "May your God, whom you serve continually, rescue you!"

A stone was brought and placed over the mouth of the den, and the king sealed it with his own signet ring and with the rings of his nobles, so that Daniel's situation might not be changed. Then the king returned to his palace and spent the night without eating and without any entertainment being brought to him. And he could not sleep.

At the first light of dawn, the king got up and hurried to the lions' den. When he came near the den, he called to Daniel in an anguished voice, "Daniel, servant of the living God, has your God, whom you serve continually, been able to rescue you from the lions?"

Daniel answered, "O king, live forever! My God sent his angel, and he shut the mouths of the lions. They have not hurt me, because I was found innocent in his sight. Nor have I ever done any wrong before you, O king."

The king was overjoyed and gave orders to lift Daniel out of the den. And when Daniel was lifted from the den, no wound was found on him, because he had trusted in his God.

At the king's command, the men who had falsely accused

Daniel were brought in and thrown into the lions' den, along with their wives and children. And before they reached the floor of the den, the lions overpowered them and crushed all their bones.

Then King Darius wrote to all the peoples, nations and men of every language throughout the land:

"May you prosper greatly!

"I issue a decree that in every part of my kingdom people must fear and reverence the God of Daniel.

"For he is the living God and he endures forever; his kingdom will not be destroyed, his dominion will never end. He rescues and he saves; he performs signs and wonders in the heavens and on the earth. He has rescued Daniel from the power of the lions."

So Daniel prospered during the reign of Darius and the reign of Cyrus the Persian. (Daniel 6:10-28)

LOOK IT OVER

3. Examine Daniel 6 carefully. What key words and ideas seem particularly important in order to understand the story? Summarize the main point of the passage in your own words.

a. Key words:

b. Key ideas:

c. Main idea:

4. List all of the traits and character qualities you observe in Daniel in this chapter.

5. Describe the trap set for Daniel by King Darius's other officials. Why did they want Daniel killed? Why did they resort to this particular trap?

6. Describe Daniel's response to their trap. Does anything surprise you about the way he responded?

THINK IT THROUGH

7. Why do you think God chose to save Daniel in such a dramatic way? How did it serve God's purposes to do so?

8. Although God miraculously delivered Daniel from persecution, He chose not to do so for many of the other godly men and women of the Bible who faced persecution (Abel was murdered by Cain, John the Baptist was executed by Herod, Stephen was stoned by the Pharisees). According to each of the following passages, why doesn't God always save His people from physical harm and difficult circumstances as He saved Daniel?

- Romans 5:3-5

- Philippians 1:18-23,27-30

- James 1:2-4

- 1 Peter 4:12-16

9. While God hasn't promised to deliver us from physical harm, He has made numerous promises to us that can give us courage even in the midst of intense persecution. What does God promise us in each of the following passages?

- Matthew 5:10-12

- Matthew 28:18-20

- Romans 8:35-39

- Revelation 2:25-27

CONVICTIONS

The desert battles of World War II were often won or lost on a few strategic hills. The side that controlled the right high ground almost always won the battle, especially if that high ground overlooked a key mountain pass or valley. Therefore, the most successful commanders were those who chose ahead of time to defend and, if necessary, to die for the right hills. They committed their men, their artillery, and even their own lives to take or defend a key section of high ground. Settling that decision before the heat of battle gave them courage and conviction to stand fast when the shells began to fall.

The trap my classmate set for me over the issue of hell turned out to be only one of the many opportunities I (Blake) had in high school to take a stand for my faith. Whether over the truthfulness of Scripture, the existence of God, or my stand on morality, my biblical beliefs and values often elicited questions and confrontation. Sometimes I responded well, standing firm for my beliefs. Sometimes I didn't. What I discovered was that just as in the desert campaigns of World War II, success hinged on choosing ahead of time on which "hills" I would die. I needed to prepare for persecution by prayerfully deciding which beliefs and practices I would take a stand for, even if it cost me.

By making those decisions ahead of time, I wasn't caught off guard when questions and ridicule came.

MAKE IT REAL

10. What beliefs and convictions do you hold that you would be willing to die for (or at least be ridiculed for)? Check any of the following, and then add your own.

    ☐ The God of the Bible exists.
    ☐ The Bible is true and reliable.
    ☐ Belief that Jesus' sacrificial death and resurrection is the *only way* to receive eternal life.
    ☐ Sexuality is to be enjoyed only within heterosexual marriage (so premarital sex, homosexual behavior, and pornography are all sinful).
    ☐ God demands honesty and integrity in all my work.
    ☐ Other: _____
    ☐ Other: _____

I would take a public stand for my belief or conviction that . . .

11. What opportunities to take a stand for your beliefs and convictions can you anticipate this week? For example, do you have a non-Christian friend or acquaintance with whom you could share your faith? Will you be around people who will gossip or speak badly about a person in authority over you? What will you do in these situations?

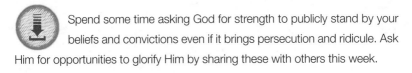

Spend some time asking God for strength to publicly stand by your beliefs and convictions even if it brings persecution and ridicule. Ask Him for opportunities to glorify Him by sharing these with others this week.

MEMORIZE

Review the previous weeks' verses, and then memorize Acts 20:24:

> **However, I consider my life worth nothing to me, if only I may finish the race and complete the task the Lord Jesus has given me — the task of testifying to the gospel of God's grace.**

Pray On!

Three times a day he got down on his knees and prayed, giving thanks to his God.

DANIEL 6:10

A NEW YORK businessman named Jeremiah Lanphier changed the world simply by starting a prayer meeting. In 1857 the world was experiencing its first international economic crisis.[1] Banks and small businesses failed. People lost their jobs, their savings, and their security. So Jeremiah began to invite other businessmen to gather at noon on Wednesdays in downtown New York to pray. Six men showed up for the first meeting, twenty for the second, then forty, then a hundred. Sensing God at work, they began to meet daily instead of weekly. Non-Christians began to come. They sought hope in the midst of the panic and found it in the good news of the gospel. As the meeting grew into the thousands, newspapers began to report on the revival. That publicity launched similar meetings throughout the United States and eventually throughout Europe. By the one-year anniversary of that first meeting, 96,216 people had accepted the gospel as a result of this growing ministry![2] In other words, one man decided to gather people together to pray during their lunch breaks and the entire world was changed as a result. Jeremiah demonstrated the truth of James 5:16, "The effective prayer of a righteous man can accomplish much" (NASB).

Daniel demonstrated that same truth many times in his life. His exceptional wisdom, integrity, and courage flowed from the deep relationship he built with God through prayer. Prayer wasn't an occasional thing for Daniel. It wasn't a last resort when all else failed. Prayer, for Daniel, was a daily discipline. Look back at the following verse from the story of the lions' den in chapter 6. Notice what it tells us about Daniel's prayer life:

> When Daniel learned that the decree had been published, he went home to his upstairs room where the windows opened toward Jerusalem. Three times a day he got down on his knees and prayed, giving thanks to his God, *just as he had done before.*
> (Daniel 6:10, emphasis added)

Fortunately, we get a glimpse into Daniel's actual prayers later in the book. He recorded one particularly emotional, heartfelt prayer in the passage below.

> I turned to the Lord God and pleaded with him in prayer and petition, in fasting, and in sackcloth and ashes.
> I prayed to the LORD my God and confessed:
> "O Lord, the great and awesome God, who keeps his covenant of love with all who love him and obey his commands, we have sinned and done wrong. We have been wicked and have rebelled; we have turned away from your commands and laws. We have not listened to your servants the prophets, who spoke in your name to our kings, our princes and our fathers, and to all the people of the land.
> "Lord, you are righteous, but this day we are covered with shame—the men of Judah and people of Jerusalem and all Israel, both near and far, in all the countries where you have

scattered us because of our unfaithfulness to you. O LORD, we and our kings, our princes and our fathers are covered with shame because we have sinned against you. The Lord our God is merciful and forgiving, even though we have rebelled against him; we have not obeyed the LORD our God or kept the laws he gave us through his servants the prophets. All Israel has transgressed your law and turned away, refusing to obey you.

"Therefore the curses and sworn judgments written in the Law of Moses, the servant of God, have been poured out on us, because we have sinned against you. You have fulfilled the words spoken against us and against our rulers by bringing upon us great disaster. Under the whole heaven nothing has ever been done like what has been done to Jerusalem. Just as it is written in the Law of Moses, all this disaster has come upon us, yet we have not sought the favor of the LORD our God by turning from our sins and giving attention to your truth. The LORD did not hesitate to bring the disaster upon us, for the LORD our God is righteous in everything he does; yet we have not obeyed him.

"Now, O Lord our God, who brought your people out of Egypt with a mighty hand and who made for yourself a name that endures to this day, we have sinned, we have done wrong. O Lord, in keeping with all your righteous acts, turn away your anger and your wrath from Jerusalem, your city, your holy hill. Our sins and the iniquities of our fathers have made Jerusalem and your people an object of scorn to all those around us.

"Now, our God, hear the prayers and petitions of your servant. For your sake, O Lord, look with favor on your desolate sanctuary. Give ear, O God, and hear; open your eyes and see the desolation of the city that bears your Name. We do not make requests of you because we are righteous, but because of your great mercy. O Lord, listen! O Lord, forgive! O Lord, hear and act! For your sake, O my God, do not delay, because your city and your people bear your Name." (Daniel 9:3-19)

1. Describe your prayer life. In what ways is it going well, and in what ways could it be better?

2. When you pray, what types of things do you say to the Lord? On what do you focus your attention?

3. Which of the following obstacles or distractions make prayer challenging for you?

- ☐ I'm just too busy.
- ☐ My mind wanders.
- ☐ I get distracted by texts, Twitter, e-mail, or something else.
- ☐ I have a hard time believing that prayer makes a difference.
- ☐ I feel too distant from God or too guilty to pray.
- ☐ I am angry at God.
- ☐ I don't have a quiet place to pray.
- ☐ Other: _____

FIGHTING TO PRAY

For many of us, prayer is a lot like eating broccoli. We know we should do it more, but we don't. We know that it is important and valuable, but we find it hard to actually sit down and pray on a regular basis.

Our difficulty with prayer shouldn't really surprise us. After all, the discipline of prayer runs counter to most of the realities and values of our modern lives. We're busy, but prayer takes time. We're distracted, but prayer takes concentration. We like instant results, but prayer takes patience. We like the loud, the fast, and the exciting, but prayer is quiet and still. We like action, but prayer demands passive dependence on God. Prayer is countercultural. To pray is to resist or even revolt against the attitudes and values of our modern world. No wonder we find prayer so challenging!

As you continue to study Daniel's prayer life, look for clues that reveal how Daniel overcame this natural struggle we have with prayer. Look closely at how he learned to prioritize prayer. Look also at the details of the prayer recorded in chapter 9 to see how he maintained focus and sincerity while speaking to the Lord.

LOOK IT OVER

4. Examine the two passages in Daniel carefully. What key words and ideas seem particularly important in order to understand these passages? In your own words, summarize the main point of the prayer in chapter 9.

   a. Key words:

   b. Key ideas:

   c. Main idea:

5. What do you notice about Daniel's prayer life in 6:10 and 9:3?

6. List all of the elements of Daniel's prayer in chapter 9. What primary ideas, themes, and requests did he include?

7. What does Daniel's prayer in chapter 9 teach us about God? In other words, what did Daniel say about God?

CRIME AND PUNISHMENT

Daniel spent most of his prayer in chapter 9 confessing his sins and the sins of his people. He did so because he knew firsthand the devastating consequences of sin. Daniel lived during the Exile, a painful time of judgment for God's people. But God's justice is not random. In the Mosaic covenant, given by God to the nation of Israel nearly a thousand years before Daniel's time, God warned His people that sin would bring judgment. The covenant promised great blessing if the Israelites obeyed the Mosaic Law, and great cursing if they did not (see Deuteronomy 28–30). After centuries of disobeying the Mosaic Law, Daniel's people justly received the ultimate form of God's curse: exile from the land. They received this curse as a result of several specific sins the prophets warned them about:

- Injustice and violence toward the vulnerable (see Isaiah 1:23)
- Trust in wealth and human strength (see Isaiah 2:6-7)
- Trust in foreign alliances (see Isaiah 31:1)
- Idolatry (see Isaiah 2:8)
- Pride (see Isaiah 2:11-12,17)

THINK IT THROUGH

8. Why would a believer like Daniel need to spend time confessing his sin? We believe that Jesus paid the full price of all of our sins, past, present, and future. So why do we need to confess our sins to the Lord? What happens if we don't? See Psalm 32:3-7 and 1 John 1:5–2:2.

9. Daniel asked God to have mercy on the Jewish people but suggested that God should do so for His own sake (see Daniel 9:17). How would providing mercy to the Jews have benefitted God (see Ezekiel 36:22-36)?

10. In his prayer in chapter 9, Daniel mentioned God's righteousness three times (see verses 7,14,16). What is God's "righteousness"? To discover what that word means, use the context of chapter 9 and look up Deuteronomy 32:4 (notice the attributes that are parallel to "righteous") and Psalm 11:7.

PRACTICAL POINTERS FOR POWERFUL PRAYER

Let us share three practical ideas that have proven especially helpful in our own prayer lives. First, think of busyness as a reason *for* prayer rather than a reason to avoid prayer. In our fast-paced, multitasking, instant-access world, we will *always* be busy. So, if you're waiting for a slow day to catch up on prayer, you may never pray again! Instead, think of that inescapable busyness as a constant reminder of your need for prayer. Who but God can help us negotiate the challenges and stresses of modern life with wisdom and integrity? Let us be able to say with the great Reformer Martin Luther, "Work, work, from morning until late at night. In fact, I have so much to do that I shall have to spend the first three hours in prayer."[3]

Second, set appointments with the Lord. Corrie ten Boom was credited as saying, "Don't pray when you feel like it. Have an appointment with the Lord and keep it. A man is powerful on his knees."[4] She's right. I rarely, if ever, miss appointments or meetings that I've taken the time to write into my calendar. If I leave it unwritten, then it's too easy to forget or to replace time for prayer when life gets busy. So add the Lord to your calendar.

Third, take advantage of "in-between" moments. The next time you're driving to work, riding the bus, walking to class, or waiting in line, resist the urge to check Twitter on your phone or listen to another song on iTunes. Instead, spend that time in prayer. If you take advantage of those moments, you'll find that you have much more time for prayer than you realized!

MAKE IT REAL

In order to pray more like Daniel, many people have found it helpful to pray through the acronym ACTS. **A** stands for "adoration" and reminds us to spend time worshipping God in prayer. Like Daniel, we should celebrate the attributes and actions of God (for example, righteous, powerful, all-knowing, good, and so forth). **C** stands for "confession" of our sins. When we confess, we consciously acknowledge that what we have done is offensive to a holy God, and that God is right in calling it sin. **T** stands for "thanksgiving." We need to constantly remind ourselves to thank God in detail for what He has done for us. Finally, **S** stands for "supplication," the act of requesting that God meet our needs and the needs of others. These include spiritual, emotional, relational, and physical needs.

11. Spend a few minutes in prayer after completing the following ACTS prayer exercise.

ACTS Prayer:
Adoration: three truths about God that I want to celebrate

Confession: sins I need God to forgive

Thanksgiving: three specific things God has done for me (spiritual, relational, material, or something else)

Supplication: specific spiritual, emotional, and physical needs

• Three things I need from the Lord

• Three things others need from the Lord

 Write down one specific way in which you can grow in the discipline of prayer. Examples: I will set an appointment with the Lord to pray for at least five minutes at 7 a.m. every day; I will create a list of people's needs so I can pray more specifically and effectively; I will turn off the radio when I'm driving to work on Monday and Wednesday mornings and spend that time in prayer.

MEMORIZE

Spend some time reviewing the verses from the previous weeks, and then memorize Colossians 4:2 (NASB):

Devote yourselves to prayer, keeping alert in it with an attitude of thanksgiving.

The Invisible War

Our struggle is not against flesh and blood, but against the rulers, against the authorities, against the powers of this dark world and against the spiritual forces of evil in the heavenly realms.

EPHESIANS 6:12

HAVE YOU EVER wondered what it would be like to sit in the Oval Office for a day and quietly watch the president in action? It would be exciting to see one of the most powerful men in the world go about his business. You would learn how he makes important decisions and you would probably hear some top-secret information.

A few years ago, the popular television show *The West Wing* attempted to pull back the curtain and show us the behind-the-scenes reality of life at the highest level of our government. Each week viewers got to watch fictional President Jed Bartlet and his staff wrestle with decisions ranging from what they should wear to a formal dinner to whether the country should declare war on another nation. The show's writers even consulted with people who had previously worked in the White House in order to make the drama as realistic as possible. During the 2001–2002 season, it was one of the top ten shows on television, proof that people are fascinated by the inner workings of powerful people.[1]

If seeing the president in action is interesting, imagine how amazing it would be to pull back the curtain on the spiritual forces at work in our universe. What if we could see angels and demons in action all around us and be fully aware of God's work in the world? Although we don't usually see it, the Bible is clear that there is a spiritual battle raging at every moment. Throughout the Bible, a few men and women were given the privilege of glimpsing the spiritual activity that typically happens beyond our view.

Daniel was one of those men. Several times, in answer to his fervent prayers for the nation of Israel, God sent an angel to talk to him directly. The angel Gabriel told Daniel about the future and even discussed the invisible war between God's angels and Satan's rebellious demons. Read Daniel 9:20-23 and 10:4-14:

> While I was speaking and praying, confessing my sin and the sin of my people Israel and making my request to the LORD my God for his holy hill—while I was still in prayer, Gabriel, the man I had seen in the earlier vision, came to me in swift flight about the time of the evening sacrifice. He instructed me and said to me, "Daniel, I have now come to give you insight and understanding. As soon as you began to pray, an answer was given, which I have come to tell you, for you are highly esteemed. Therefore, consider the message and understand the vision." . . .
>
> On the twenty-fourth day of the first month, as I was standing on the bank of the great river, the Tigris, I looked up and there before me was a man dressed in linen, with a belt of the finest gold around his waist. His body was like chrysolite, his face like lightning, his eyes like flaming torches, his arms and legs like the gleam of burnished bronze, and his voice like the sound of a multitude.
>
> I, Daniel, was the only one who saw the vision; the men with me did not see it, but such terror overwhelmed them that they fled and hid themselves. So I was left alone, gazing at this

great vision; I had no strength left, my face turned deathly pale and I was helpless. Then I heard him speaking, and as I listened to him, I fell into a deep sleep, my face to the ground.

A hand touched me and set me trembling on my hands and knees. He said, "Daniel, you who are highly esteemed, consider carefully the words I am about to speak to you, and stand up, for I have now been sent to you." And when he said this to me, I stood up trembling.

Then he continued, "Do not be afraid, Daniel. Since the first day that you set your mind to gain understanding and to humble yourself before your God, your words were heard, and I have come in response to them. But the prince of the Persian kingdom resisted me twenty-one days. Then Michael, one of the chief princes, came to help me, because I was detained there with the king of Persia. Now I have come to explain to you what will happen to your people in the future, for the vision concerns a time yet to come."

CONSIDERING THE SPIRITUAL WORLD

1. When you hear the words *spiritual warfare*, what comes to your mind? Are there movies, music, art, or books that have impacted your thinking on the subject?

2. Why do you think there are so many books and movies about angels and demons these days?

LOOK IT OVER

Popular movies and television shows often portray spiritual warfare as a battle between two equally powerful beings, God and Satan. In reality, Scripture tells us that God is infinitely more powerful than His enemies. He will win in the end and cast the Devil into the lake of fire for eternity (see Revelation 20:10). However, Daniel learned that Satan's forces won't go down without a fight. Although he will not win the war, Satan hopes to wreak as much destruction as possible right now, so that you and I will not know or serve God well. Daniel gives us a glimpse into the tactics the Devil uses to try to thwart God's purposes in the world.

3. Examine Daniel 9:20-23 and 10:4-14 carefully. What key words and ideas seem particularly important in order to understand the stories? Summarize the main point of the passages in your own words.

   a. Key words:

   b. Key ideas:

   c. Main idea:

4. What happened in the spiritual realm when Daniel prayed? Describe how the forces of God and the forces of evil were involved in the events of chapters 9–10.

5. The Bible mentions the angel Gabriel on several occasions (see Daniel 8:16; 9:21; Luke 1:19,26). What did he do on God's behalf?

»»
WHAT IS AN ANGEL?

The English word *angel* comes from a Greek word that means "messenger." God created angels before the world began (see Job 38:7), and carrying messages from God is one of their primary tasks. For example, Gabriel carried God's prophetic message to Daniel. He also told Zechariah about the birth of his son John the Baptist and of the coming Messiah (see Luke 1:8-23). But angels serve other purposes as well. For example, God used an angel to destroy Israel's enemies (see Isaiah 37:36). Angels called cherubim and seraphim surround God's throne and constantly worship Him (see Isaiah 6:1-7). When Daniel was in the lions' den, God sent an angel to protect him, and angels ministered to Jesus on the night before His crucifixion (see Luke 22:43). To summarize, angels are simply God's messengers and ministers. They exist to worship Him, spread His messages, wage war on His enemies, and support His people.

6. The archangel Michael is mentioned a number of times as well (see Daniel 10:13,21; Jude 9; Revelation 12:7). What did he do on God's behalf?

MORE THAN MEETS THE EYE

One of the more dramatic illustrations of spiritual warfare in the Bible is recorded in 2 Kings 6:8-23. The king of Aram was at war with Israel, and he was losing badly. The prophet Elisha was supernaturally predicting his every move and reporting it to the king of Israel. So the king of Aram decided to capture Elisha. He sent a huge force of soldiers to surround the prophet and arrest him.

When Elisha's servant saw the army surrounding them, he was terrified. But Elisha simply replied, "Don't be afraid. . . . Those who are with us are more than those who are with them" (verse 16). He then prayed that God would open his servant's eyes to see the spiritual reality around them. The servant looked around and saw the hills covered with God's forces—horses and chariots of fire that outnumbered the enemy. God's forces blinded the opposing soldiers and sent them home in defeat.

Elisha's servant must have felt overwhelmed when he saw the angels of God protecting him. Daniel may have felt the same way when Gabriel appeared to him and revealed God's future plans for the nation of Israel. Although Israel's future seemed bleak, God had a plan and a power that wasn't visible to the naked eye. Both stories are a good reminder that God's plans are often much greater than we can understand, and the power available to us through prayer and obedience is much greater than we can imagine.

THINK IT THROUGH

7. What do you think was the reason for the battle between God's angels and the prince of Persia? What was each of them trying to accomplish?

8. Why do you think Daniel's prayers were answered so clearly and dramatically? Why doesn't God always answer our prayers that way?

9. Read the following passages. What tactics does Satan use in his attempts to destroy God's work in the world?

   • John 8:44

   • Zechariah 3:1-2

   • Mark 4:14-15

- 2 Corinthians 11:14-15

- 1 John 3:8-10

10. Read Ephesians 6:11-18. What weapons has God provided for us so that we can counter the tactics of Satan and his demons?

MAKE IT REAL

Every football coach knows the value of studying the opposition. Each week, the coach watches videos of his opponent's games. He studies their offensive and defensive strategies. He learns any tricks the other team might use to misdirect and confuse his own players. He then shares his findings with his team so that they can be prepared to win. A good coach will even design the team's practices based on what he's learned from watching the film. By doing so, he can prepare his players to respond well on the field to their particular opponent.

In much the same way, the Bible tells us about the strategies of our enemy, Satan. God also gives us weapons and tools to counter Satan's tactics. We looked at Satan's strategies and God's tools in the "Think It Through" section. Now let's apply this information directly to our lives.

11. Look at the list you made above of Satan's tactics. To which of them are you most vulnerable?

12. We saw in John 8:44 that one of Satan's primary strategies is to lie to God's people. The following is a list of common lies the Enemy tells us. Check the ones you're most tempted to believe. If there are others, write them in the space provided.

- ☐ God can't use me because I'm too sinful.
- ☐ Maybe God isn't even real.
- ☐ The Bible can't be trusted.
- ☐ I'm not smart enough or gifted enough to make any difference for God.
- ☐ I can't serve God until I accomplish other important goals in my life (such as getting married, finding a good job, finishing school).
- ☐ I can't trust God with my life because He won't do what's best for me.
- ☐ This life might be all there really is, so I should pursue my own happiness and pleasure rather than God's will.
- ☐ I've worked really hard to be good this week, so I deserve just this one little sin.
- ☐ Other: _____

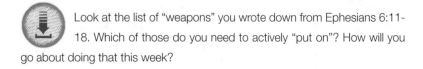

Look at the list of "weapons" you wrote down from Ephesians 6:11-18. Which of those do you need to actively "put on"? How will you go about doing that this week?

13. Spend some time alone or with your group asking God for the strength to resist the Devil and fight His battles well.

MEMORIZE

Review last week's verse, and then memorize Ephesians 6:10-11:

Finally, be strong in the Lord and in his mighty power. Put on the full armor of God so that you can take your stand against the devil's schemes.

Living Today in Light of Forever

Do this, understanding the present time. The hour has come for you to wake up from your slumber, because our salvation is nearer now than when we first believed.

ROMANS 13:11

NOTHING RUINS A student's day as quickly as a pop quiz, especially in hard subjects like calculus or chemistry. Without warning, students often show up unprepared and end up discouraged and frustrated. In fact, at the college we three attended, Texas A&M University, students could actually research professors before signing up for classes in order to avoid those who favored this cruel form of examination! Not surprisingly, we favored the professors who gave their classes plenty of warning about upcoming quizzes. The best professors, in our humble opinion, told you not only when the quiz would be, but what information would be covered. If you arrived on test day inadequately prepared, you would have no one to blame but yourself.

»»»

JUST KEEP IT TO YOURSELF . . .

Imagine receiving information on Friday evening that none of your classmates knew. On Monday morning, your teacher was planning a surprise examination that would count for 100 percent of your grade for the semester. How would that information change your weekend plans? Would you tell anyone else, or would you keep the secret to yourself? Would you tell only your friends, or would you tell your rivals as well?

Throughout history, God has acted much like our favorite professors: He has gone out of His way to prepare people for the tests and trials of life. One of the tools He has given us is prophecy: writings of Scripture that declare what God intends to do in the future. These prophetic writings, to which Daniel made a significant contribution, benefit us in three crucial ways. First, when prophecies are fulfilled, they strengthen our faith in a God who knows and controls the future. Second, they give us strength to resist sin by helping us understand the serious future consequences of disobedience. Finally, they give us courage to boldly follow God in the present by showing us the rewarding and satisfying future that awaits those who walk in faith.

The book of Daniel contains many prophecies, some of which have already been fulfilled and some of which will be fulfilled in the future. We'll look at the most famous of his predictions, a prophecy Daniel received from the angel Gabriel concerning God's plan for the nation of Israel.

While I was speaking and praying, confessing my sin and the sin of my people Israel and making my request to the LORD my God for his holy hill—while I was still in prayer, Gabriel, the man I had seen in the earlier vision, came to me in swift flight about the time of the evening sacrifice. He instructed me and said to me, "Daniel, I have now come to give you insight and understanding. As soon as you began to pray, an answer was given, which I have come to tell you, for you are highly esteemed. Therefore, consider the message and understand the vision:

"Seventy 'sevens' are decreed for your people and your holy city to finish transgression, to put an end to sin, to atone for wickedness, to bring in everlasting righteousness, to seal up vision and prophecy and to anoint the most holy.

"Know and understand this: From the issuing of the decree to restore and rebuild Jerusalem until the Anointed One, the ruler, comes, there will be seven 'sevens,' and sixty-two 'sevens.' It will be rebuilt with streets and a trench, but in times of trouble. After the sixty-two 'sevens,' the Anointed One will be cut off and will have nothing. The people of the ruler who will come will destroy the city and the sanctuary. The end will come like a flood: War will continue until the end, and desolations have been decreed. He will confirm a covenant with many for one 'seven.' In the middle of the 'seven' he will put an end to sacrifice and offering. And on a wing of the temple he will set up an abomination that causes desolation, until the end that is decreed is poured out on him." (Daniel 9:20-27)

SEVENTY "SEVENS"? WHAT'S UP WITH BIBLE MATH?

Most of Daniel's prophecies are challenging to figure out, and this one is no exception! The key is knowing that by "sevens" (or literally "weeks"), God is referring to periods of seven years. In other words, God is telling Daniel that from the issuing of a king's decree to rebuild Jerusalem, 483 years (7 sevens + 62 sevens) will pass until the Anointed One (literally, "the Messiah") will arrive. Daniel received this prophecy from Gabriel around the year 539 BC.[1] Nearly a century later, on March 5, 444 BC,[2] a Persian king named Artaxerxes issued a surprising decree allowing the Jews to rebuild their capital city. (Kings rarely allowed a conquered people to rebuild a city's defensive walls, as it would strengthen their ability to rebel.) Then, exactly 483 years later, on March 30, AD 33, Jesus, rode into Jerusalem on a donkey and was hailed as God's Messiah-King, just as Daniel had predicted. The prophecy proved true in exact detail.[3]

1. What comes to mind when you hear the word *prophecy?* What prophecies from the Bible are you familiar with?

2. Do you see any practical benefit to biblical prophecy? In other words, how would your life be different if God had included no prophecy in the Bible?

3. Fulfilled prophecy can strengthen our confidence in God. Look up each of the following prophecies from the Old Testament. What exactly did God predict in each passage?

   • Micah 5:2

   • Psalm 22:14-18

   • Isaiah 45:1-7,13 (spoken 150 years before Cyrus was born!)

FULFILLED PROPHECY: DANIEL 2

Daniel 2 is a prophecy of the future ruling powers of the earth. Daniel interpreted the following list of kingdoms and the time periods of their power as they aligned with the parts of the statue in King Nebuchadnezzar's dream.[4]

Head of gold:
Babylonia (605–539 BC)

Chest and arms of silver:
Medo-Persia (539–332 BC);
see Daniel 8:20

Belly and thighs of bronze:
Greece (332–63 BC);
see Daniel 8:21

Legs of iron and feet
of iron and clay:
Rome (63 BC–AD 476)

Stone/Mountain: God's kingdom

LOOK IT OVER

4. Examine Daniel 9:20-27 carefully. What key words and ideas seem particularly important in order to understand the story? Summarize the main point of the passage in your own words.

   a. Key words:

   b. Key ideas:

   c. Main idea:

5. Using verses 26-27, list everything that will happen to Daniel's people after the Anointed One is "cut off."

6. How do you think Daniel felt after hearing the prophecy in verses 20-27 — encouraged, fearful, a combination of the two feelings? Why?

SPOILER ALERT!

Brian and I (Blake) love to backpack in the Rocky Mountains, and we always carry a map and a compass. Getting lost in the midst of thousands of square miles of wilderness is not a pleasant experience. And even when you know right where you are, it's helpful to know what's coming next.

A topographical trail map helps you plan your route carefully. You know what changes in elevation to prepare for — steep climbs and abrupt descents requiring ropes. You know what hazards to avoid — high cliffs and raging rivers.

Likewise, biblical prophecy enables God's people to prepare wisely for the future. God doesn't want us wandering through life in the dark. He wants us well prepared and well equipped for every challenge and opportunity the future holds. And so, in books like Daniel, God fills us in on what's to come. He gives us a preview of the last pages of the book of human history. We see ahead of time the world-changing events that will accompany the "last days" of this world.

One of those events is described in detail in the final verse of our passage in Daniel 9. You may have noticed that of the seventy "sevens" that Gabriel spoke of, only sixty-nine occurred between the decree to rebuild Jerusalem and the death of the Messiah. What about the last "seven," or the last period of seven years? That's described in verse 27. When Israel rejected Jesus as their Messiah, God put His "seventy 'sevens'" plan for Israel on pause. He began a new work through a new people, the church. But in the future, God will return to His plan for the nation of Israel, and it will begin with a painful seven years of persecution called the Great Tribulation, described in verse 27. The "ruler who will come" (verse 26) refers to a powerful world ruler the New Testament calls the antichrist (see 1 John 2:18). He will make a covenant with the "many," referring to Daniel's people, the Israelites. But midway through the tribulation he will break that covenant, outlaw the religious practices of the Jews, desecrate their temple, and begin a program of persecution against them. However, at the end of the seven years, he himself will be utterly destroyed. As Revelation 19:11-21 reveals in greater detail, his destruction will come at the hands of Jesus, the Anointed One, who will return in terrifying power to annihilate His enemies and deliver His people. In other words, despite the appearance of defeat (being "cut off" in the Crucifixion), Jesus will win in the end.

THINK IT THROUGH

7. This particular prophecy came through an angelic mediator, Gabriel. How else did God give prophecies in the book of Daniel (see 2:28-29; 5:4-12; 7:1-3)?

8. According to each of the following passages, why is it reasonable to entrust your life and your future to the prophecies of Scripture?

- 2 Timothy 3:16-17

- 2 Peter 1:20-21

9. What has God revealed about our future in each of the
following passages?

- Isaiah 2:2-4

- Isaiah 65:17-25

- Daniel 12:1-3

- Revelation 20:11-15

- Revelation 21:1-7

»»
WHAT'S NEXT?

Because prophecy can be challenging to interpret, Christians often
disagree on exactly what will occur in the future. Yet most agree that
Jesus Christ will return to the earth and establish His kingdom, just as
He promised (see Matthew 25:31-34). In fact, Daniel predicted that
the kingdom of God would overwhelm and replace all human kingdoms (see Daniel 2:44-45; 7:13-14) and that God's people would
reign forever with Him (see Daniel 7:18).

Based on our understanding of Daniel and other prophetic
books, we believe that God has a number of events in store for the
future of this world. They are outlined in the chart on the next page.

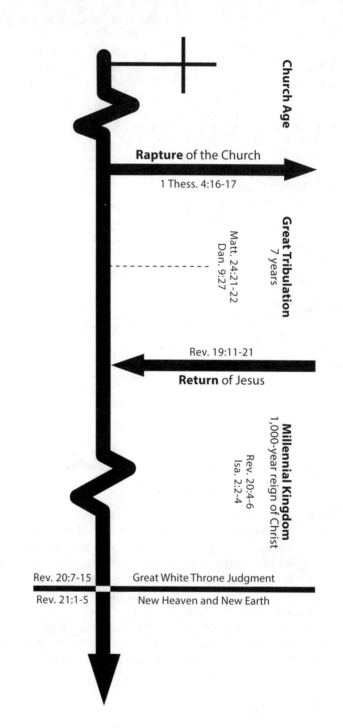

Church Age

Rapture of the Church

1 Thess. 4:16-17

Great Tribulation
7 years

Matt. 24:21-22
Dan. 9:27

Rev. 19:11-21
Return of Jesus

Millennial Kingdom
1,000-year reign of Christ

Rev. 20:4-6
Isa. 2:2-4

Rev. 20:7-15   Great White Throne Judgment
Rev. 21:1-5   New Heaven and New Earth

MAKE IT REAL

10. Does knowing the end of the story of human history give you comfort or fear? Why? (Note: Daniel felt more fear than comfort when he received visions and dreams.)

~~~~~~

Read Romans 13:11-14. If Jesus were to return tomorrow to establish God's kingdom on earth, would you be ready? Complete the following activity to identify steps you need to take to be ready for that day.

I will pursue the following changes in my life by the power of God's Spirit in order to prepare for Jesus Christ's return:

☐ I will avoid _____ by
_____.

☐ I will begin _____ by
_____.

☐ I will . . .

~~~~~~

11. Read 2 Peter 3:7-15. How should our knowledge of the future change our attitudes and interactions with people who don't have a personal relationship with God through faith in Jesus Christ?

Daniel and his friends proved to be remarkable examples of the power of one's convictions. They withstood the temptations and abuse of a hostile culture, and as a result of their fortitude, they opened the eyes of many to the surpassing greatness of the one true God. We face similar threats with similar opportunities to stand strong and bear witness to the power of our God. Take a few minutes to review the lessons you have learned. Ask God to strengthen you with the courage to stand strong and bring Him honor in your world.

MEMORIZE

Review the verses from the previous weeks, and then memorize 2 Peter 3:14:

> **So then, dear friends, since you are looking forward to this, make every effort to be found spotless, blameless and at peace with him.**

Leader's Guide

WE'RE GLAD THAT you've decided to lead your group through this study of the life of Daniel and his friends. We pray that God will use this study to transform you and the students in your group into more faithful servants of Him. The Word of God really can change us for the better when we study it together and challenge each other to obey it.

The degree to which a small group understands and applies Scripture ultimately depends on the work of the Holy Spirit. However, the leader has a critical role in helping the group listen carefully to God's Word. Your role, then, is to constantly point your group back to Scripture and challenge them to understand and apply it. As you guide your group through the main passages of Scripture and additional verses of the study, be sure participants each have a Bible so they can fully engage with the Word.

LESSON FORMAT

Each lesson of this study is broken down into four major sections (this format is loosely based on the inductive Bible study methodology outlined in *Living by the Book*, by Howard and William Hendricks[1]):

Introduction/Need: Every lesson begins with an opening story designed to stir interest in the subject and to relate the main point of the passage to a real-life situation. Following the written introduction, we have included a few questions to provoke some initial thought about the week's topic. Our goal in this section is simply to help the group see the need to study the passage and to introduce perhaps one or two ways in which the passage might be personally relevant.

Look It Over: This section is designed to stimulate observation directly from the text. The purpose of these questions is not to inquire about the *meaning* of the text (the next section will accomplish that goal), but instead just to observe what the passage actually *says*. As a leader, you'll want to continually challenge the group to ground their observations in the biblical text. One temptation at this stage will be for you or other group members to jump ahead to application. For example, Daniel was given several prophecies regarding future events. Members of your group might feel inclined to immediately ask, "How does our knowledge of future events help us in our daily relationships with God and others?" However, that is an application question. Save those types of questions for the final section, "Make It Real." Instead, at this stage focus on questions related to the text itself, such as "What specific future events were revealed to Daniel?" or "What types of visual images did God use to reveal future events?" By studying the passage carefully, your group will be better prepared to understand and apply it.

Think It Through: This portion of the study is designed to take students deeper into the text through the process of interpretation. Sometimes we need to answer difficult questions before we can apply the text. For instance, the world of the Bible was quite different from our own. As a result, you might need to walk your group through a bit of background study or look up a few cross-references. Where necessary, we've provided dialogue boxes with critical information to help you in this process. For example, in the third lesson it helps to know the meaning of the word *integrity* when discussing character. Continue to resist the temptation to apply the text at this point; instead, help your group understand what it means (not what it means *to you or to the students* but what it actually means *in light of the original context*).

Make It Real: The final section of each lesson is designed to encourage personal application of the text. Every passage of Scripture, even those that seem the strangest to us today, contains principles that are timeless and can be applied to our lives. To that end, we've provided questions and exercises to prompt the students to reflect on their own lives, identify where they are falling short, and make a specific plan for growth. Don't let your group members leave their applications general ("I will be more thankful to God"); help them make specific, concrete plans ("I will grow in thankfulness by spending at least five minutes a day each day this week writing down specific things I am thankful to God for"). As the leader, consider organizing group activities for some of the applications. Students (especially young men) often connect with one another and learn best in an active setting, so you might plan service projects, road trips, or other similar events to help with the application process. We also encourage group accountability. Don't allow the applications to be forgotten after the discussion for each lesson, but instead return to them in subsequent weeks to help your group hold one another accountable.

At the end of each lesson, we have included a memory verse. We encourage you to have your group members recite these each week. However, if memorizing all of the verses is too overwhelming, pick one or two and focus on them throughout the course of the study.

STRUCTURING YOUR TIME

Depending on the topic, the composition of your group, and their level of preparation, your group time might be structured in several different ways. We recommend that you allow at least an hour for your group meetings, and more time if possible. Assuming that your group has about an hour to meet, here is a suggested timeline (adjust this proportionately if you have more or less time each week):

5–10 minutes: Welcome and prayer
5–10 minutes: Introduction/Need
10–15 minutes: Look It Over
15–20 minutes: Think It Through
10–15 minutes: Make It Real

We recognize that it is often challenging to answer all of the questions in your allotted time. If one question or concept generates a great deal of discussion, it's not always wise to end the dialogue simply to move on to the next question. As the leader, use your discretion to determine whether to allow a "rabbit trail" or to gently encourage the group to move on to a different topic. Consider carefully whether a particular discussion is the most productive use of time for the entire group. If an issue is troubling one member more than the others, offer to meet with him or her individually at a different time. That will allow you to continue with the study in a way that meets the needs of all members.

Nothing energizes a Bible study like challenging questions. Though we've included many questions in the book, we encourage you to go beyond them. Brainstorm questions of your own from the passage to ask your group. Include "devil's advocate" questions in which you take a counter-position and force your group to defend their views from Scripture. Many students, especially guys, love debate, so don't hesitate to dial up the tension in your meetings! In our own groups we like to create "healthy tension"—just enough is left unanswered so that group members are motivated to dig deeper on their own, but not so much that they feel discouraged and disoriented by a lack of answers to their questions.

If your group has not prepared ahead of time, begin by reading the lesson's passage(s) with them, and encouraging them to verbally make observations. You might want to provide some initial observations and thoughts on the passage for your group just to get them started. You can write their observations on a dry-erase board, project them onto a screen, or have the group members write in their own books. After spending a few minutes observing, challenge them to answer the most critical questions from "Think It Through" on the spot. Finally, prompt them to think through how they might apply the text this coming week.

Most important, do not skip the "Make It Real" portion of the study in the interest of time. Ultimately, the effectiveness of a Bible study is measured by the impact it has on the group members' lives, not by the knowledge it generates. If you are short on time, move quickly through the "Look It Over" and "Think It Through" sections so you have time to discuss applications.

THEMES AND KEY QUESTIONS FOR EACH WEEK

Daniel is an exceptionally dense piece of Scripture that can and should be studied for a lifetime. And although limitless lessons can be gleaned from his prophecies and experiences, our primary focus in this study is on how Daniel's life, and the lives of his companions, challenge us to stand strong and maintain our integrity even when it could cost us greatly. Daniel, Hananiah, Mishael, and Azariah were placed in circumstances that easily could have caused them to become resentful and compromise their beliefs. Instead, relying on God, His revealed Word, and one another, they chose faithfulness. As a result, these four young men revealed to the Babylonians, even to the king himself, the nature and attributes of the one true God. Rather than becoming conformed to their new world, they had a lasting impact. Their legacy can become our legacy as we resolve to live by God's power and for His glory.

Each lesson of the study contributes to that idea in a different way. Here are the themes and critical questions to answer for each lesson of the study:

Lesson 1: The study begins by establishing the historical setting of the book—in particular, the experience of exile in which the four young men were living. Make sure you become familiar with the timeline. You will probably want to mark this page and come back to it frequently throughout the study. The historical setting is critical for understanding the rest of the book of Daniel. Suffering is a pretty straightforward concept for most people to understand. However, watch out for "disconnect" in two possible ways. First, some of your group members, if they are young, may never have suffered much (physical suffering, persecution, peer pressure, and so forth). Help them relate by connecting to the experience of others in the group. Second, some of your group members may be completely preoccupied with their sufferings and want to dominate the discussion by telling their stories. Help the group connect to Daniel's experience and then move them on. Our response to present suffering and our preparation for future suffering is most important. Focus the group's attention on ways we can respond to suffering so that we can grow in character rather than become bitter. The questions based on James 1 (8 and 9) will be very useful. Help members understand the distinction between happiness (completely based on circumstances) and joy (which transcends circumstances).

Lesson 2: The world tries to conform us to its values, but sometimes its methods are so subtle that we fail to recognize their impact on us. This lesson is designed to help us not only understand the world's values, but also live more intentionally and with self-awareness. Critical to this process is identifying the world's false gods that people worship—first in the context of ancient Babylon, and then in our own culture. These false gods are universal and timeless. The connection between Daniel's world and ours should become obvious. Questions 7 through 10 will help you lead your group from understanding the concept of a personal name, to a culture's promotion of false gods, to a value system that is destructive. Before wrapping up this lesson, make sure you spend some time discussing what is *true*. In other words, it is not enough to identify what is false; we must replace it with what is true. Together, look up several of the verses in question 11. Encourage your group members to list other truths of God's Word that help us combat the false worldview of our culture.

Lesson 3: This lesson focuses on integrity, or—to put it in the negative—moral compromise. Of course, in this world a price must always be paid for maintaining our integrity. However, it strengthens us to realize that the price is small when compared to what we forfeit when we fail to take a stand for what we believe in. No one ever feels good in the end about compromise. Spend time at the beginning of the lesson helping your group members understand the significance of the king's food and drink in historical context. A casual reading of this story could lead someone to think, "What's the big deal? Why didn't they just eat the king's food? It probably tasted better than vegetables!" However, this was a real temptation to moral compromise. For the application of this lesson, your members should think ahead about the kinds of temptations to compromise they face, the proper response to each temptation, and their resolution to stand firm in their integrity. Spend some time encouraging them through the examples of biblical characters in question 10. Knowing that others have succeeded under similar, or even more difficult, temptations can greatly strengthen our resolve.

Lesson 4: This lesson challenges students to connect with a strong Christian community in order to stand strong in their faith. The key idea to emphasize is that walking with God is not a solitary endeavor, but that we all need friends and encouragement from others. Shadrach, Meshach, and Abednego are great biblical examples of this principle. Question 13 gives some other examples that will be helpful for your group to consider. The biblical passage is particularly long in this lesson, so we've divided it into two sections for observation. Don't overlook either part, because both are critical to understanding the story. Also, spend some time on tougher theological issues, like question 11 about the fourth man in the fire, and question 12 about the state of mind of the three young Hebrew men as they faced the fire. The "Make It Real" section might be challenging for some students, especially if they don't have a solid group of Christian friends. Pray for them, and gently encourage them to actively participate at church and to ask God to provide for them. Do your best to facilitate this community within your group, as well. Consider hosting dinner at your home or taking your group for a fun activity followed by a time of prayer and study. It might even be a good idea to pair them up for prayer and accountability throughout the week.

Lesson 5: The main idea of this lesson is courage in the face of persecution. Even though most of us will probably never face potential martyrdom for our faith, we will have to pay a price for our faithfulness to Christ. This lesson prepares us to face persecution with courage and faithfulness just as Daniel did. In the "Look It Over" section, focus on questions 4 and 6 to get a better sense of Daniel's character in action.

Under "Think It Through," you'll need to spend some time on questions 8 and 9. God has not promised to deliver us from the consequences of persecution. He may do so as He did for Daniel. Or He may not if there is a greater good that persecution can accomplish. But we can have great hope because God has promised that even if persecution comes, He will stay with us in the midst of it (see Matthew 28), He will hold us fast in His love (see Romans 8), and He will reward us in eternity if we stay faithful in persecution (see Matthew 5; Revelation 2). Make sure to leave sufficient time for questions 11 and 12. Question 11 is especially important because if we don't choose ahead of time what beliefs and convictions to suffer for we will buckle when persecution comes. Spend time sharing the additional beliefs and convictions your group members listed. Also, have group members share times when they suffered for these beliefs. How did they respond? How could they do better in the future?

Lesson 6: The goal of this lesson is to learn from Daniel how to pray effectively and powerfully by prioritizing prayer in one's daily life. Your group members should come to see prayer as the most important, valuable use of their time. And they should leave with practical ideas for how to improve both the quality and quantity of their prayers. As you go through the lesson, focus on questions 1 and 2. Encourage your group to honestly assess their prayer lives. You can't make improvements until you've identified what needs to be improved. Then spend some time on questions 5 through 7 by simply listing all that the text tells us in answer to these questions. This is a great opportunity to practice the skill of observation. Under "Think It Through," make sure to discuss question 8. Once we trust in the gospel, our eternal life is absolutely secure. We can't lose it even if we sin and even if we fail to confess it (see Romans 8:35-39). But confession *is* required if we want to enjoy our relationship with God and experience His power, peace, and joy. As 1 John 1 makes clear, it's impossible to walk with God in the light (enjoy fellowship with Him) if we hold on to unconfessed sin. Leave plenty of time for question 11 and the download activity. You may want to do question 11 together since some of your group members may have little experience praying in this holistic way. And make sure everyone leaves with a personal application from the download activity.

Lesson 7: This lesson is designed to make your group members more aware of the spiritual battle that rages around us every day. Even though we can't see them, angels and demons are real and are active in our world. Through prayer and obedience to God, we have the opportunity to participate in that battle and to be a part of what God is doing to defeat His enemies. Daniel's life is a vivid illustration of the power of prayer in the spiritual realm, so this lesson gives you the chance to highlight that theme in his life. Make sure you spend time in the "Look It Over" and "Think It Through" sections discussing the reality of angels and demons as opposed to the perceptions of them we receive from our culture. Most important, though, talk about the schemes of the Devil to lie to God's people, and the weapons we have from Ephesians 6:11-18 to fight against those schemes. Each group member should walk away from this lesson knowing which of Satan's schemes pose particular threats to him or her and having concrete ways to counter those tactics. Strongly encourage your group toward prayer, accountability, Scripture memory, and Christian community.

Lesson 8: No study of Daniel would be complete without an overview of prophecy, since Daniel's prophecies take up most of the book. In this lesson, we use the prophecy revealed at the end of chapter 9 to teach us the value of studying biblical prophecy and to introduce us to some of the future events in store for us. Spend time on the introductory questions, especially questions 2 and 3. Prepare to help your group really grasp the incredible, practical benefit that biblical prophecy can have in our lives (it can give us hope, confidence, courage, and more). Also, spend significant time on questions 8 and 9. On question 9, after listing what each passage tells us about the future, ask your group why any of this matters. Do these future events affect their daily lives in any way? Again, your goal is to help them see that these promises from God can give us great hope (believers have a *great* future in store), great courage

(I can take risks now knowing that God will deliver and reward me in the future), and great compassion (what a terrifying future awaits those who do not trust in Jesus!). You may find it helpful to talk through the chart in the "What's Next?" call-out box. Don't worry if you don't agree with all the events we've listed—godly believers have always disagreed about the details of prophecy. Simply present your view and let others present theirs. Finally, spend good time on the download activity and question 11. Make sure all of your group members leave with a clear, concrete application in mind. Prophecy is useless to us unless we apply it!

"STAND STRONG!"

May God give you courage to stand strong in a hostile world, just as He strengthened Daniel and his friends. We pray that God will bring honor to Himself through you and that together your group will grow closer to the Lord as you experience the transforming power of godly friends and fellowship. We're confident that His Spirit will be at work in your group as you are faithful to consistently direct them to His Word. For further resources, take a look at Grace Bible Church's website, www.grace-bible.org, or contact NavPress at www.navpress.com. And don't forget to check out the other studies in the ORDINARY GREATNESS series.

Notes

LESSON 1: WHY ME, GOD?

1. Eugene Merrill, *Kingdom of Priests* (Grand Rapids, MI: Baker, 1987), 192, 320, 452, 469, 502–503, 514.
2. "The Ten Boom Family," Ten Boom Museum, http://tenboom.org/aboutthetenboomsc48.php.
3. "Corrie ten Boom," PBS, http://www.pbs.org/wgbh/questionofgod/voices/boom.html.

LESSON 2: HELLO, MY NAME IS . . .

1. Gleason Archer, *The Expositor's Bible Commentary,* ed. Frank E. Gaebelein, vol. 7 (Grand Rapids, MI: Zondervan, 1985), s.v. "Daniel," 32, 34–35.
2. A. C. Myers, *The Eerdmans Bible Dictionary* (Grand Rapids, MI: Eerdmans, 1987), s.v. "Babylonia," 118.
3. Myers, s.v. "Babylonia."
4. W. A. Elwell and P. W. Comfort, *Tyndale Bible Dictionary*, Tyndale Reference Library (Wheaton, IL: Tyndale, 2001), s.v. "Babylon; Babylonia," 139.
5. Elwell, s.v. "Babylon; Babylonia."

LESSON 3: NO COMPROMISE

1. Walter A. Elwell and Barry J. Beitzel, *Baker Encyclopedia of the Bible* (Grand Rapids, MI: Baker, 1988), 538.

LESSON 4: STRENGTH IN NUMBERS

1. "Forty Martyrs of Sebaste," Wikipedia, http://en.wikipedia.org/wiki/Forty_Martyrs_of_Sebaste#Veneration_in_the_East.

LESSON 5: STANDING (AND KNEELING) ALONE

1. "Tsavo Maneaters," Wikipedia, http://en.wikipedia.org/wiki/Tsavo
_maneaters; "Lions of Tsavo," fieldmuseum.org, http://archive
.fieldmuseum.org/exhibits/exhibit_sites/tsavo/default.htm; James Henry
Patterson, *The Man-Eaters of Tsavo and Other East African Adventures*
(Minneapolis: Filiquarian Publishing, 2006), 67.

LESSON 6: PRAY ON!

1. "Panic of 1857," Wikipedia, http://en.wikipedia.org/wiki/Panic_of_1857.
2. Wesley L. Duewel, *Revival Fire* (Grand Rapids, MI: Zondervan, 2010),
128–130.
3. Martin Luther, quoted in Edward Bounds, *Purpose in Prayer* (Radford, VA:
Wilder Publications, 2008), 13.
4. Corrie ten Boom, quoted in Becky Tirabassi, *One Year Sacred Obsession
Devotional* (Wheaton, IL: Tyndale, 2007), 7.

LESSON 7: THE INVISIBLE WAR

1. "The West Wing," Wikipedia, http://en.wikipedia.org/wiki/
The_West_Wing#Nielsen_ratings.

LESSON 8: LIVING TODAY IN LIGHT OF FOREVER

1. J. F. Walvoord, R. B. Zuck, and Dallas Theological Seminary, *The Bible
Knowledge Commentary: An Exposition of the Scriptures* (Wheaton, IL:
Victor, 1983), s.v. Daniel 9:1.
2. *The Bible Knowledge Commentary*, s.v. Daniel 9:25.
3. Harold Hoehner, *Chronological Aspects of the Life of Christ* (Grand Rapids,
MI: Zondervan, 1978), 138.
4. *The Bible Knowledge Commentary*, s.v. Daniel 2:36-45a.

LEADER'S GUIDE

1. Howard and William Hendricks, *Living by the Book* (Chicago: Moody,
1991).

About the Authors

Brian Fisher, Matt Morton, and Blake Jennings serve together at Grace Bible Church in College Station, Texas. GBC is a multisite church of four thousand people located near Texas A&M University. Because of the church's focus on the next generation of spiritual leaders, more than two thousand students attend weekly college worship times and participate in weekly Bible studies, discipleship, and summer missions opportunities.

Brian serves as the senior pastor of GBC. He holds a master's degree and a doctorate from Dallas Theological Seminary and is a graduate of Texas A&M University. He is married to Tristie. They have two beautiful children.

Matt is the college pastor of GBC's Anderson Campus. He graduated from Dallas Theological Seminary and Texas A&M University. He and his wife, Shannon, have three wonderful children.

Blake is the teaching pastor of GBC's Southwood Campus. He graduated from Dallas Theological Seminary and Texas A&M University. He and his wife, Julie, are the proud parents of Gracie and Luke.